PASS WORD CRYPT O- CLUE

DATABOOK

ublisher: Kitonya Kompany, Tallahassee, Florida USA.
 ISBN-13

isclaimer: We strongly advise against the recording of financial or any other highly personal information in this databook. he owner of this record is solely responsible for the information stored within. Do not share your key with anyone. We ecommend disposal of key upon memorization. **Please use responsibly**.

Welcome to Password Crypto-Clue

Are you ready to stop 'P-O'? P-O is Password Overload and millions of people are experiencing it. It is a well known fact that the average person has accumulated almost 100 different passwords for 100 different sites and gadgets. On top of that, we have to constantly change these passwords for security and other reasons which require more time and mental storage. But writing down real passwords in today's cybercrime environment is a big taboo, and most people will not risk sharing their biometrics online, so what else is there?

That's where Password Crypto-Clue comes in. Password Crypto-Clue is the perfect solution for securing your passwords while also freeing your mind from the clutter of Password Overload. Using only the characters on your QWERTY keyboard, Password Crypto-Clue provides you with a flexible Matrix Key that you change in any way you choose to create your own unique Encryption/Decryption clues for all your password needs. Now you can stop P-O with P-C.

How to use Password Crypto-Clue:

There are several different versions of Cryptography which utilize encryption to prevent unauthorized access to sensitive information. We use a form of Cryptography we call Substitution Crypto-Clue where the characters of your real password are substituted with letters, numbers, or symbols. You Encode your real password using your own unique Crypto-Clues or Clue Keys (examples are on the next page) and write this encrypted password into your password book. When you log into a site, you Decode your encrypted password (examples are on the next page) and type your real decrypted password into the site. Whenever you see your Clue Keys in an encrypted password, you know to do a substitution. This way you never have to write down your real passwords, and you only have to remember ONE STRING OF CLUE KEYS that you created instead of 100 Passwords, too easy!

Follow our Crypto-Clue examples on the next page. Review the encoded text and read how to decode it following our Substitution Matrix Key. Try to decode the last encoded text yourself, before checking the decrypted answer in the back of the book. Have fun!

SUBSTITUTION CRYPTO-CLUE MATRIX KEY

Key Mate Number/Symbol	!	@	#	$	%	^	&	*	(	)
	1	2	3	4	5	6	7	8	9	0

Underlined text in Encoded means — Use CAPS to Decode
Brackets on Encoded Number/Symbol mean — Use Corresponding Key Mate to Decode
Strikethrough text in Encoded means — Delete Text to Decode
Plus Symbol in Encoded text means — Insert 10-4 to Decode

Examples for Underlined text

(ENCODED) samiam *write in book* — (DECODED) SamIam *type in computer*

(ENCODED) samiam — (DECODED) saMiaM

Examples for Brackets text

(ENCODED) sam[1]am — (DECODED) sam!am

(ENCODED) samiam[@] — (DECODED) samiam2

Examples for Strikethrough text

(ENCODED) samiam~~too~~ — (DECODED) samiam

(ENCODED) ~~sam~~iamtoo — (DECODED) iamtoo

Examples for Plus Symbol text

(ENCODED) sam+iam — (DECODED) sam10-4iam

(ENCODED) samiam+ — (DECODED) samiam10-4

Example for Combination Crypto-Clue text

(ENCODED) ~~sa~~miam?[3]+ — (Decoded answer in back of book)

WEBSITE: www.kitonyakompany.com

USER ID: Kitonya

CRYPTOCLUE: +admin1[123]

MISC: acct #5551212

A

WEBSITE:

USER ID:

CRYPTOCLUE:

MISC:

WEBSITE:

USER ID:

CRYPTOCLUE:

MISC:

WEBSITE:

USER ID:

CRYPTOCLUE:

MISC:

WEBSITE:

USER ID:

CRYPTOCLUE:

MISC:

WEBSITE:

USER ID:

CRYPTOCLUE:

MISC:

WEBSITE:

USER ID:

CRYPTOCLUE:

MISC:

WEBSITE:

USER ID:

CRYPTOCLUE:

MISC:

WEBSITE:

USER ID:

CRYPTOCLUE:

MISC:

A

WEBSITE:

USER ID:

CRYPTOCLUE:

MISC:

WEBSITE:

USER ID:

CRYPTOCLUE:

MISC:

WEBSITE:

USER ID:

CRYPTOCLUE:

MISC:

WEBSITE:

USER ID:

CRYPTOCLUE:

MISC:

WEBSITE:
USER ID:
CRYPTOCLUE:
MISC:

WEBSITE:
USER ID:
CRYPTOCLUE:
MISC:

WEBSITE:
USER ID:
CRYPTOCLUE:
MISC:

WEBSITE:
USER ID:
CRYPTOCLUE:
MISC:

A

WEBSITE:

USER ID:

CRYPTOCLUE:

MISC:

WEBSITE:

USER ID:

CRYPTOCLUE:

MISC:

WEBSITE:

USER ID:

CRYPTOCLUE:

MISC:

WEBSITE:

USER ID:

CRYPTOCLUE:

MISC:

B

WEBSITE:

USER ID:

CRYPTOCLUE:

MISC:

WEBSITE:

USER ID:

CRYPTOCLUE:

MISC:

WEBSITE:

USER ID:

CRYPTOCLUE:

MISC:

WEBSITE:

USER ID:

CRYPTOCLUE:

MISC:

B

WEBSITE:

USER ID:

CRYPTOCLUE:

MISC:

WEBSITE:

USER ID:

CRYPTOCLUE:

MISC:

WEBSITE:

USER ID:

CRYPTOCLUE:

MISC:

WEBSITE:

USER ID:

CRYPTOCLUE:

MISC:

WEBSITE:

USER ID:

CRYPTOCLUE:

MISC:

WEBSITE:

USER ID:

CRYPTOCLUE:

MISC:

WEBSITE:

USER ID:

CRYPTOCLUE:

MISC:

WEBSITE:

USER ID:

CRYPTOCLUE:

MISC:

B

WEBSITE:

USER ID:

CRYPTOCLUE:

MISC:

WEBSITE:

USER ID:

CRYPTOCLUE:

MISC:

WEBSITE:

USER ID:

CRYPTOCLUE:

MISC:

WEBSITE:

USER ID:

CRYPTOCLUE:

MISC:

WEBSITE:

USER ID:

CRYPTOCLUE:

MISC:

WEBSITE:

USER ID:

CRYPTOCLUE:

MISC:

WEBSITE:

USER ID:

CRYPTOCLUE:

MISC:

WEBSITE:

USER ID:

CRYPTOCLUE:

MISC:

C

WEBSITE:

USER ID:

CRYPTOCLUE:

MISC:

WEBSITE:

USER ID:

CRYPTOCLUE:

MISC:

WEBSITE:

USER ID:

CRYPTOCLUE:

MISC:

WEBSITE:

USER ID:

CRYPTOCLUE:

MISC:

WEBSITE:

USER ID:

CRYPTOCLUE:

MISC:

WEBSITE:

USER ID:

CRYPTOCLUE:

MISC:

WEBSITE:

USER ID:

CRYPTOCLUE:

MISC:

WEBSITE:

USER ID:

CRYPTOCLUE:

MISC:

C

WEBSITE:

USER ID:

CRYPTOCLUE:

MISC:

WEBSITE:

USER ID:

CRYPTOCLUE:

MISC:

WEBSITE:

USER ID:

CRYPTOCLUE:

MISC:

WEBSITE:

USER ID:

CRYPTOCLUE:

MISC:

WEBSITE:

USER ID:

CRYPTOCLUE:

MISC:

WEBSITE:

USER ID:

CRYPTOCLUE:

MISC:

WEBSITE:

USER ID:

CRYPTOCLUE:

MISC:

WEBSITE:

USER ID:

CRYPTOCLUE:

MISC:

D

WEBSITE:

USER ID:

CRYPTOCLUE:

MISC:

WEBSITE:

USER ID:

CRYPTOCLUE:

MISC:

WEBSITE:

USER ID:

CRYPTOCLUE:

MISC:

WEBSITE:

USER ID:

CRYPTOCLUE:

MISC:

WEBSITE:

USER ID:

CRYPTOCLUE:

MISC:

WEBSITE:

USER ID:

CRYPTOCLUE:

MISC:

WEBSITE:

USER ID:

CRYPTOCLUE:

MISC:

WEBSITE:

USER ID:

CRYPTOCLUE:

MISC:

D

WEBSITE:

USER ID:

CRYPTOCLUE:

MISC:

WEBSITE:

USER ID:

CRYPTOCLUE:

MISC:

WEBSITE:

USER ID:

CRYPTOCLUE:

MISC:

WEBSITE:

USER ID:

CRYPTOCLUE:

MISC:

WEBSITE:

USER ID:

CRYPTOCLUE:

MISC:

WEBSITE:

USER ID:

CRYPTOCLUE:

MISC:

WEBSITE:

USER ID:

CRYPTOCLUE:

MISC:

WEBSITE:

USER ID:

CRYPTOCLUE:

MISC:

E

WEBSITE:

USER ID:

CRYPTOCLUE:

MISC:

WEBSITE:

USER ID:

CRYPTOCLUE:

MISC:

WEBSITE:

USER ID:

CRYPTOCLUE:

MISC:

WEBSITE:

USER ID:

CRYPTOCLUE:

MISC:

WEBSITE:

USER ID:

CRYPTOCLUE:

MISC:

WEBSITE:

USER ID:

CRYPTOCLUE:

MISC:

WEBSITE:

USER ID:

CRYPTOCLUE:

MISC:

WEBSITE:

USER ID:

CRYPTOCLUE:

MISC:

E

WEBSITE:

USER ID:

CRYPTOCLUE:

MISC:

WEBSITE:

USER ID:

CRYPTOCLUE:

MISC:

WEBSITE:

USER ID:

CRYPTOCLUE:

MISC:

WEBSITE:

USER ID:

CRYPTOCLUE:

MISC:

WEBSITE:

USER ID:

CRYPTOCLUE:

MISC:

WEBSITE:

USER ID:

CRYPTOCLUE:

MISC:

WEBSITE:

USER ID:

CRYPTOCLUE:

MISC:

WEBSITE:

USER ID:

CRYPTOCLUE:

MISC:

F

WEBSITE:

USER ID:

CRYPTOCLUE:

MISC:

WEBSITE:

USER ID:

CRYPTOCLUE:

MISC:

WEBSITE:

USER ID:

CRYPTOCLUE:

MISC:

WEBSITE:

USER ID:

CRYPTOCLUE:

MISC:

WEBSITE:

USER ID:

CRYPTOCLUE:

MISC:

WEBSITE:

USER ID:

CRYPTOCLUE:

MISC:

WEBSITE:

USER ID:

CRYPTOCLUE:

MISC:

WEBSITE:

USER ID:

CRYPTOCLUE:

MISC:

F

WEBSITE:

USER ID:

CRYPTOCLUE:

MISC:

WEBSITE:

USER ID:

CRYPTOCLUE:

MISC:

WEBSITE:

USER ID:

CRYPTOCLUE:

MISC:

WEBSITE:

USER ID:

CRYPTOCLUE:

MISC:

WEBSITE:

USER ID:

CRYPTOCLUE:

MISC:

WEBSITE:

USER ID:

CRYPTOCLUE:

MISC:

WEBSITE:

USER ID:

CRYPTOCLUE:

MISC:

WEBSITE:

USER ID:

CRYPTOCLUE:

MISC:

G

WEBSITE:

USER ID:

CRYPTOCLUE:

MISC:

WEBSITE:

USER ID:

CRYPTOCLUE:

MISC:

WEBSITE:

USER ID:

CRYPTOCLUE:

MISC:

WEBSITE:

USER ID:

CRYPTOCLUE:

MISC:

WEBSITE:

USER ID:

CRYPTOCLUE:

MISC:

WEBSITE:

USER ID:

CRYPTOCLUE:

MISC:

WEBSITE:

USER ID:

CRYPTOCLUE:

MISC:

WEBSITE:

USER ID:

CRYPTOCLUE:

MISC:

G

WEBSITE:

USER ID:

CRYPTOCLUE:

MISC:

WEBSITE:

USER ID:

CRYPTOCLUE:

MISC:

WEBSITE:

USER ID:

CRYPTOCLUE:

MISC:

WEBSITE:

USER ID:

CRYPTOCLUE:

MISC:

WEBSITE:

USER ID:

CRYPTOCLUE:

MISC:

WEBSITE:

USER ID:

CRYPTOCLUE:

MISC:

WEBSITE:

USER ID:

CRYPTOCLUE:

MISC:

WEBSITE:

USER ID:

CRYPTOCLUE:

MISC:

H

WEBSITE:

USER ID:

CRYPTOCLUE:

MISC:

WEBSITE:

USER ID:

CRYPTOCLUE:

MISC:

WEBSITE:

USER ID:

CRYPTOCLUE:

MISC:

WEBSITE:

USER ID:

CRYPTOCLUE:

MISC:

WEBSITE:

USER ID:

CRYPTOCLUE:

MISC:

WEBSITE:

USER ID:

CRYPTOCLUE:

MISC:

WEBSITE:

USER ID:

CRYPTOCLUE:

MISC:

WEBSITE:

USER ID:

CRYPTOCLUE:

MISC:

H

WEBSITE:

USER ID:

CRYPTOCLUE:

MISC:

WEBSITE:

USER ID:

CRYPTOCLUE:

MISC:

WEBSITE:

USER ID:

CRYPTOCLUE:

MISC:

WEBSITE:

USER ID:

CRYPTOCLUE:

MISC:

WEBSITE:

USER ID:

CRYPTOCLUE:

MISC:

WEBSITE:

USER ID:

CRYPTOCLUE:

MISC:

WEBSITE:

USER ID:

CRYPTOCLUE:

MISC:

WEBSITE:

USER ID:

CRYPTOCLUE:

MISC:

I

WEBSITE:

USER ID:

CRYPTOCLUE:

MISC:

WEBSITE:

USER ID:

CRYPTOCLUE:

MISC:

WEBSITE:

USER ID:

CRYPTOCLUE:

MISC:

WEBSITE:

USER ID:

CRYPTOCLUE:

MISC:

WEBSITE:

USER ID:

CRYPTOCLUE:

MISC:

WEBSITE:

USER ID:

CRYPTOCLUE:

MISC:

WEBSITE:

USER ID:

CRYPTOCLUE:

MISC:

WEBSITE:

USER ID:

CRYPTOCLUE:

MISC:

I

WEBSITE:

USER ID:

CRYPTOCLUE:

MISC:

WEBSITE:

USER ID:

CRYPTOCLUE:

MISC:

WEBSITE:

USER ID:

CRYPTOCLUE:

MISC:

WEBSITE:

USER ID:

CRYPTOCLUE:

MISC:

WEBSITE:

USER ID:

CRYPTOCLUE:

MISC:

WEBSITE:

USER ID:

CRYPTOCLUE:

MISC:

WEBSITE:

USER ID:

CRYPTOCLUE:

MISC:

WEBSITE:

USER ID:

CRYPTOCLUE:

MISC:

J

WEBSITE:

USER ID:

CRYPTOCLUE:

MISC:

WEBSITE:

USER ID:

CRYPTOCLUE:

MISC:

WEBSITE:

USER ID:

CRYPTOCLUE:

MISC:

WEBSITE:

USER ID:

CRYPTOCLUE:

MISC:

WEBSITE:

USER ID:

CRYPTOCLUE:

MISC:

WEBSITE:

USER ID:

CRYPTOCLUE:

MISC:

WEBSITE:

USER ID:

CRYPTOCLUE:

MISC:

WEBSITE:

USER ID:

CRYPTOCLUE:

MISC:

J

WEBSITE:

USER ID:

CRYPTOCLUE:

MISC:

WEBSITE:

USER ID:

CRYPTOCLUE:

MISC:

WEBSITE:

USER ID:

CRYPTOCLUE:

MISC:

WEBSITE:

USER ID:

CRYPTOCLUE:

MISC:

K

WEBSITE:

USER ID:

CRYPTOCLUE:

MISC:

WEBSITE:

USER ID:

CRYPTOCLUE:

MISC:

WEBSITE:

USER ID:

CRYPTOCLUE:

MISC:

WEBSITE:

USER ID:

CRYPTOCLUE:

MISC:

K

WEBSITE:

USER ID:

CRYPTOCLUE:

MISC:

WEBSITE:

USER ID:

CRYPTOCLUE:

MISC:

WEBSITE:

USER ID:

CRYPTOCLUE:

MISC:

WEBSITE:

USER ID:

CRYPTOCLUE:

MISC:

WEBSITE:

USER ID:

CRYPTOCLUE:

MISC:

WEBSITE:

USER ID:

CRYPTOCLUE:

MISC:

WEBSITE:

USER ID:

CRYPTOCLUE:

MISC:

WEBSITE:

USER ID:

CRYPTOCLUE:

MISC:

K

WEBSITE:

USER ID:

CRYPTOCLUE:

MISC:

WEBSITE:

USER ID:

CRYPTOCLUE:

MISC:

WEBSITE:

USER ID:

CRYPTOCLUE:

MISC:

WEBSITE:

USER ID:

CRYPTOCLUE:

MISC:

WEBSITE:

USER ID:

CRYPTOCLUE:

MISC:

WEBSITE:

USER ID:

CRYPTOCLUE:

MISC:

WEBSITE:

USER ID:

CRYPTOCLUE:

MISC:

WEBSITE:

USER ID:

CRYPTOCLUE:

MISC:

L

WEBSITE:

USER ID:

CRYPTOCLUE:

MISC:

WEBSITE:

USER ID:

CRYPTOCLUE:

MISC:

WEBSITE:

USER ID:

CRYPTOCLUE:

MISC:

WEBSITE:

USER ID:

CRYPTOCLUE:

MISC:

L

WEBSITE:

USER ID:

CRYPTOCLUE:

MISC:

WEBSITE:

USER ID:

CRYPTOCLUE:

MISC:

WEBSITE:

USER ID:

CRYPTOCLUE:

MISC:

WEBSITE:

USER ID:

CRYPTOCLUE:

MISC:

L

WEBSITE:

USER ID:

CRYPTOCLUE:

MISC:

WEBSITE:

USER ID:

CRYPTOCLUE:

MISC:

WEBSITE:

USER ID:

CRYPTOCLUE:

MISC:

WEBSITE:

USER ID:

CRYPTOCLUE:

MISC:

WEBSITE:

USER ID:

CRYPTOCLUE:

MISC:

WEBSITE:

USER ID:

CRYPTOCLUE:

MISC:

WEBSITE:

USER ID:

CRYPTOCLUE:

MISC:

WEBSITE:

USER ID:

CRYPTOCLUE:

MISC:

M

WEBSITE:

USER ID:

CRYPTOCLUE:

MISC:

WEBSITE:

USER ID:

CRYPTOCLUE:

MISC:

WEBSITE:

USER ID:

CRYPTOCLUE:

MISC:

WEBSITE:

USER ID:

CRYPTOCLUE:

MISC:

WEBSITE:

USER ID:

CRYPTOCLUE:

MISC:

WEBSITE:

USER ID:

CRYPTOCLUE:

MISC:

WEBSITE:

USER ID:

CRYPTOCLUE:

MISC:

WEBSITE:

USER ID:

CRYPTOCLUE:

MISC:

M

WEBSITE:

USER ID:

CRYPTOCLUE:

MISC:

WEBSITE:

USER ID:

CRYPTOCLUE:

MISC:

WEBSITE:

USER ID:

CRYPTOCLUE:

MISC:

WEBSITE:

USER ID:

CRYPTOCLUE:

MISC:

WEBSITE:

USER ID:

CRYPTOCLUE:

MISC:

WEBSITE:

USER ID:

CRYPTOCLUE:

MISC:

WEBSITE:

USER ID:

CRYPTOCLUE:

MISC:

WEBSITE:

USER ID:

CRYPTOCLUE:

MISC:

N

WEBSITE:

USER ID:

CRYPTOCLUE:

MISC:

WEBSITE:

USER ID:

CRYPTOCLUE:

MISC:

WEBSITE:

USER ID:

CRYPTOCLUE:

MISC:

WEBSITE:

USER ID:

CRYPTOCLUE:

MISC:

N

WEBSITE:

USER ID:

CRYPTOCLUE:

MISC:

WEBSITE:

USER ID:

CRYPTOCLUE:

MISC:

WEBSITE:

USER ID:

CRYPTOCLUE:

MISC:

WEBSITE:

USER ID:

CRYPTOCLUE:

MISC:

N

WEBSITE:

USER ID:

CRYPTOCLUE:

MISC:

WEBSITE:

USER ID:

CRYPTOCLUE:

MISC:

WEBSITE:

USER ID:

CRYPTOCLUE:

MISC:

WEBSITE:

USER ID:

CRYPTOCLUE:

MISC:

O

WEBSITE:

USER ID:

CRYPTOCLUE:

MISC:

WEBSITE:

USER ID:

CRYPTOCLUE:

MISC:

WEBSITE:

USER ID:

CRYPTOCLUE:

MISC:

WEBSITE:

USER ID:

CRYPTOCLUE:

MISC:

O

WEBSITE:

USER ID:

CRYPTOCLUE:

MISC:

WEBSITE:

USER ID:

CRYPTOCLUE:

MISC:

WEBSITE:

USER ID:

CRYPTOCLUE:

MISC:

WEBSITE:

USER ID:

CRYPTOCLUE:

MISC:

O

WEBSITE:

USER ID:

CRYPTOCLUE:

MISC:

WEBSITE:

USER ID:

CRYPTOCLUE:

MISC:

WEBSITE:

USER ID:

CRYPTOCLUE:

MISC:

WEBSITE:

USER ID:

CRYPTOCLUE:

MISC:

O

WEBSITE:

USER ID:

CRYPTOCLUE:

MISC:

WEBSITE:

USER ID:

CRYPTOCLUE:

MISC:

WEBSITE:

USER ID:

CRYPTOCLUE:

MISC:

WEBSITE:

USER ID:

CRYPTOCLUE:

MISC:

WEBSITE:

USER ID:

CRYPTOCLUE:

MISC:

WEBSITE:

USER ID:

CRYPTOCLUE:

MISC:

WEBSITE:

USER ID:

CRYPTOCLUE:

MISC:

WEBSITE:

USER ID:

CRYPTOCLUE:

MISC:

P

WEBSITE:

USER ID:

CRYPTOCLUE:

MISC:

WEBSITE:

USER ID:

CRYPTOCLUE:

MISC:

WEBSITE:

USER ID:

CRYPTOCLUE:

MISC:

WEBSITE:

USER ID:

CRYPTOCLUE:

MISC:

WEBSITE:

USER ID:

CRYPTOCLUE:

MISC:

WEBSITE:

USER ID:

CRYPTOCLUE:

MISC:

WEBSITE:

USER ID:

CRYPTOCLUE:

MISC:

WEBSITE:

USER ID:

CRYPTOCLUE:

MISC:

P

WEBSITE:

USER ID:

CRYPTOCLUE:

MISC:

WEBSITE:

USER ID:

CRYPTOCLUE:

MISC:

WEBSITE:

USER ID:

CRYPTOCLUE:

MISC:

WEBSITE:

USER ID:

CRYPTOCLUE:

MISC:

WEBSITE:

USER ID:

CRYPTOCLUE:

MISC:

WEBSITE:

USER ID:

CRYPTOCLUE:

MISC:

WEBSITE:

USER ID:

CRYPTOCLUE:

MISC:

WEBSITE:

USER ID:

CRYPTOCLUE:

MISC:

Q

WEBSITE:

USER ID:

CRYPTOCLUE:

MISC:

WEBSITE:

USER ID:

CRYPTOCLUE:

MISC:

WEBSITE:

USER ID:

CRYPTOCLUE:

MISC:

WEBSITE:

USER ID:

CRYPTOCLUE:

MISC:

WEBSITE:

USER ID:

CRYPTOCLUE:

MISC:

WEBSITE:

USER ID:

CRYPTOCLUE:

MISC:

WEBSITE:

USER ID:

CRYPTOCLUE:

MISC:

WEBSITE:

USER ID:

CRYPTOCLUE:

MISC:

Q

WEBSITE:

USER ID:

CRYPTOCLUE:

MISC:

WEBSITE:

USER ID:

CRYPTOCLUE:

MISC:

WEBSITE:

USER ID:

CRYPTOCLUE:

MISC:

WEBSITE:

USER ID:

CRYPTOCLUE:

MISC:

WEBSITE:

USER ID:

CRYPTOCLUE:

MISC:

WEBSITE:

USER ID:

CRYPTOCLUE:

MISC:

WEBSITE:

USER ID:

CRYPTOCLUE:

MISC:

WEBSITE:

USER ID:

CRYPTOCLUE:

MISC:

R

WEBSITE:

USER ID:

CRYPTOCLUE:

MISC:

WEBSITE:

USER ID:

CRYPTOCLUE:

MISC:

WEBSITE:

USER ID:

CRYPTOCLUE:

MISC:

WEBSITE:

USER ID:

CRYPTOCLUE:

MISC:

WEBSITE:

USER ID:

CRYPTOCLUE:

MISC:

WEBSITE:

USER ID:

CRYPTOCLUE:

MISC:

WEBSITE:

USER ID:

CRYPTOCLUE:

MISC:

WEBSITE:

USER ID:

CRYPTOCLUE:

MISC:

R

WEBSITE:

USER ID:

CRYPTOCLUE:

MISC:

WEBSITE:

USER ID:

CRYPTOCLUE:

MISC:

WEBSITE:

USER ID:

CRYPTOCLUE:

MISC:

WEBSITE:

USER ID:

CRYPTOCLUE:

MISC:

WEBSITE:

USER ID:

CRYPTOCLUE:

MISC:

WEBSITE:

USER ID:

CRYPTOCLUE:

MISC:

WEBSITE:

USER ID:

CRYPTOCLUE:

MISC:

WEBSITE:

USER ID:

CRYPTOCLUE:

MISC:

S

WEBSITE:

USER ID:

CRYPTOCLUE:

MISC:

WEBSITE:

USER ID:

CRYPTOCLUE:

MISC:

WEBSITE:

USER ID:

CRYPTOCLUE:

MISC:

WEBSITE:

USER ID:

CRYPTOCLUE:

MISC:

WEBSITE:

USER ID:

CRYPTOCLUE:

MISC:

WEBSITE:

USER ID:

CRYPTOCLUE:

MISC:

WEBSITE:

USER ID:

CRYPTOCLUE:

MISC:

WEBSITE:

USER ID:

CRYPTOCLUE:

MISC:

S

WEBSITE:

USER ID:

CRYPTOCLUE:

MISC:

WEBSITE:

USER ID:

CRYPTOCLUE:

MISC:

WEBSITE:

USER ID:

CRYPTOCLUE:

MISC:

WEBSITE:

USER ID:

CRYPTOCLUE:

MISC:

WEBSITE:

USER ID:

CRYPTOCLUE:

MISC:

WEBSITE:

USER ID:

CRYPTOCLUE:

MISC:

WEBSITE:

USER ID:

CRYPTOCLUE:

MISC:

WEBSITE:

USER ID:

CRYPTOCLUE:

MISC:

T

WEBSITE:

USER ID:

CRYPTOCLUE:

MISC:

WEBSITE:

USER ID:

CRYPTOCLUE:

MISC:

WEBSITE:

USER ID:

CRYPTOCLUE:

MISC:

WEBSITE:

USER ID:

CRYPTOCLUE:

MISC:

WEBSITE:

USER ID:

CRYPTOCLUE:

MISC:

WEBSITE:

USER ID:

CRYPTOCLUE:

MISC:

WEBSITE:

USER ID:

CRYPTOCLUE:

MISC:

WEBSITE:

USER ID:

CRYPTOCLUE:

MISC:

T

WEBSITE:

USER ID:

CRYPTOCLUE:

MISC:

WEBSITE:

USER ID:

CRYPTOCLUE:

MISC:

WEBSITE:

USER ID:

CRYPTOCLUE:

MISC:

WEBSITE:

USER ID:

CRYPTOCLUE:

MISC:

WEBSITE:

USER ID:

CRYPTOCLUE:

MISC:

WEBSITE:

USER ID:

CRYPTOCLUE:

MISC:

WEBSITE:

USER ID:

CRYPTOCLUE:

MISC:

WEBSITE:

USER ID:

CRYPTOCLUE:

MISC:

U

WEBSITE:

USER ID:

CRYPTOCLUE:

MISC:

WEBSITE:

USER ID:

CRYPTOCLUE:

MISC:

WEBSITE:

USER ID:

CRYPTOCLUE:

MISC:

WEBSITE:

USER ID:

CRYPTOCLUE:

MISC:

U

WEBSITE:

USER ID:

CRYPTOCLUE:

MISC:

WEBSITE:

USER ID:

CRYPTOCLUE:

MISC:

WEBSITE:

USER ID:

CRYPTOCLUE:

MISC:

WEBSITE:

USER ID:

CRYPTOCLUE:

MISC:

U

WEBSITE:

USER ID:

CRYPTOCLUE:

MISC:

WEBSITE:

USER ID:

CRYPTOCLUE:

MISC:

WEBSITE:

USER ID:

CRYPTOCLUE:

MISC:

WEBSITE:

USER ID:

CRYPTOCLUE:

MISC:

WEBSITE:

USER ID:

CRYPTOCLUE:

MISC:

WEBSITE:

USER ID:

CRYPTOCLUE:

MISC:

WEBSITE:

USER ID:

CRYPTOCLUE:

MISC:

WEBSITE:

USER ID:

CRYPTOCLUE:

MISC:

V

WEBSITE:

USER ID:

CRYPTOCLUE:

MISC:

WEBSITE:

USER ID:

CRYPTOCLUE:

MISC:

WEBSITE:

USER ID:

CRYPTOCLUE:

MISC:

WEBSITE:

USER ID:

CRYPTOCLUE:

MISC:

WEBSITE:

USER ID:

CRYPTOCLUE:

MISC:

WEBSITE:

USER ID:

CRYPTOCLUE:

MISC:

WEBSITE:

USER ID:

CRYPTOCLUE:

MISC:

WEBSITE:

USER ID:

CRYPTOCLUE:

MISC:

V

WEBSITE:

USER ID:

CRYPTOCLUE:

MISC:

WEBSITE:

USER ID:

CRYPTOCLUE:

MISC:

WEBSITE:

USER ID:

CRYPTOCLUE:

MISC:

WEBSITE:

USER ID:

CRYPTOCLUE:

MISC:

WEBSITE:

USER ID:

CRYPTOCLUE:

MISC:

WEBSITE:

USER ID:

CRYPTOCLUE:

MISC:

WEBSITE:

USER ID:

CRYPTOCLUE:

MISC:

WEBSITE:

USER ID:

CRYPTOCLUE:

MISC:

W

WEBSITE:

USER ID:

CRYPTOCLUE:

MISC:

WEBSITE:

USER ID:

CRYPTOCLUE:

MISC:

WEBSITE:

USER ID:

CRYPTOCLUE:

MISC:

WEBSITE:

USER ID:

CRYPTOCLUE:

MISC:

WEBSITE:

USER ID:

CRYPTOCLUE:

MISC:

WEBSITE:

USER ID:

CRYPTOCLUE:

MISC:

WEBSITE:

USER ID:

CRYPTOCLUE:

MISC:

WEBSITE:

USER ID:

CRYPTOCLUE:

MISC:

W

WEBSITE:

USER ID:

CRYPTOCLUE:

MISC:

WEBSITE:

USER ID:

CRYPTOCLUE:

MISC:

WEBSITE:

USER ID:

CRYPTOCLUE:

MISC:

WEBSITE:

USER ID:

CRYPTOCLUE:

MISC:

WEBSITE:

USER ID:

CRYPTOCLUE:

MISC:

WEBSITE:

USER ID:

CRYPTOCLUE:

MISC:

WEBSITE:

USER ID:

CRYPTOCLUE:

MISC:

WEBSITE:

USER ID:

CRYPTOCLUE:

MISC:

X

WEBSITE:

USER ID:

CRYPTOCLUE:

MISC:

WEBSITE:

USER ID:

CRYPTOCLUE:

MISC:

WEBSITE:

USER ID:

CRYPTOCLUE:

MISC:

WEBSITE:

USER ID:

CRYPTOCLUE:

MISC:

X

WEBSITE:

USER ID:

CRYPTOCLUE:

MISC:

WEBSITE:

USER ID:

CRYPTOCLUE:

MISC:

WEBSITE:

USER ID:

CRYPTOCLUE:

MISC:

WEBSITE:

USER ID:

CRYPTOCLUE:

MISC:

X

WEBSITE:

USER ID:

CRYPTOCLUE:

MISC:

WEBSITE:

USER ID:

CRYPTOCLUE:

MISC:

WEBSITE:

USER ID:

CRYPTOCLUE:

MISC:

WEBSITE:

USER ID:

CRYPTOCLUE:

MISC:

WEBSITE:

USER ID:

CRYPTOCLUE:

MISC:

WEBSITE:

USER ID:

CRYPTOCLUE:

MISC:

WEBSITE:

USER ID:

CRYPTOCLUE:

MISC:

WEBSITE:

USER ID:

CRYPTOCLUE:

MISC:

Y

WEBSITE:

USER ID:

CRYPTOCLUE:

MISC:

WEBSITE:

USER ID:

CRYPTOCLUE:

MISC:

WEBSITE:

USER ID:

CRYPTOCLUE:

MISC:

WEBSITE:

USER ID:

CRYPTOCLUE:

MISC:

Y

WEBSITE:

USER ID:

CRYPTOCLUE:

MISC:

WEBSITE:

USER ID:

CRYPTOCLUE:

MISC:

WEBSITE:

USER ID:

CRYPTOCLUE:

MISC:

WEBSITE:

USER ID:

CRYPTOCLUE:

MISC:

Y

WEBSITE:

USER ID:

CRYPTOCLUE:

MISC:

WEBSITE:

USER ID:

CRYPTOCLUE:

MISC:

WEBSITE:

USER ID:

CRYPTOCLUE:

MISC:

WEBSITE:

USER ID:

CRYPTOCLUE:

MISC:

WEBSITE:

USER ID:

CRYPTOCLUE:

MISC:

WEBSITE:

USER ID:

CRYPTOCLUE:

MISC:

WEBSITE:

USER ID:

CRYPTOCLUE:

MISC:

WEBSITE:

USER ID:

CRYPTOCLUE:

MISC:

Z

WEBSITE:

USER ID:

CRYPTOCLUE:

MISC:

WEBSITE:

USER ID:

CRYPTOCLUE:

MISC:

WEBSITE:

USER ID:

CRYPTOCLUE:

MISC:

WEBSITE:

USER ID:

CRYPTOCLUE:

MISC:

WEBSITE:

USER ID:

CRYPTOCLUE:

MISC:

WEBSITE:

USER ID:

CRYPTOCLUE:

MISC:

WEBSITE:

USER ID:

CRYPTOCLUE:

MISC:

WEBSITE:

USER ID:

CRYPTOCLUE:

MISC:

Z

WEBSITE:

USER ID:

CRYPTOCLUE:

MISC:

WEBSITE:

USER ID:

CRYPTOCLUE:

MISC:

WEBSITE:

USER ID:

CRYPTOCLUE:

MISC:

WEBSITE:

USER ID:

CRYPTOCLUE:

MISC:

NOTES

NOTES

NOTES

NOTES

(Decoded Answer) amIam?#10-4

Pro Tip: Make only as many Clue Keys as you can remember

Made in the USA
Monee, IL
04 November 2026

67378020R00066